Body Books

Blood

Anna Sandeman
Illustrated by Ian Thompson

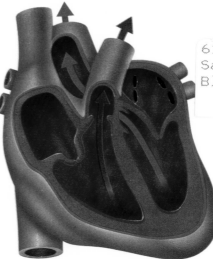

COPPER BEECH BOOKS
BROOKFIELD, CONNECTICUT

Copyright © 1996 Aladdin Books Ltd.
Produced by Aladdin Books Limited
28 Percy Street
London W1P 0LD

Designed by: David West Children's
Book Design
Designer: Edward Simkins
Editor: Liz White
Picture Research: Brooks Krikler Research
Consultants: Dr. R. Levene, M.D.
Jan Bastoncino, Dip. Ed.

First published in
the United States in 1996 by
Copper Beech Books,
an imprint of The Millbrook Press
2 Old New Milford Road
Brookfield, Connecticut 06804

Printed in Belgium

**Library of Congress Cataloging-in-Publication
Data**
Sandeman, Anna.
Blood / by Anna Sandeman; illustrated by Ian
Thompson.
p. cm. – (Body books)
Includes index.
Summary: Explains what blood is, what it does, and how
it circulates in the human body.
ISBN 0-7613-0477-0 (lib. bdg.)
1. Blood–Juvenile literature. [1. Blood.] I. Thompson, Ian,
1964- ill. II. Title. III. Series:
Sandeman, Anna. Body books.
QP91.S23 1996
612.1'1–dc20   95-40834
                     CIP AC

Photocredits
Abbreviations: t-top, m-middle, b-bottom, r-right, l-left
All the pictures are by Roger Vlitos apart from the following pages;
19 & 27 - Science Photo Library; 22-23, 26 & 29br - Frank Spooner
Pictures; 28-29 - Spectrum 28b - Mary Evans Picture Library

Contents

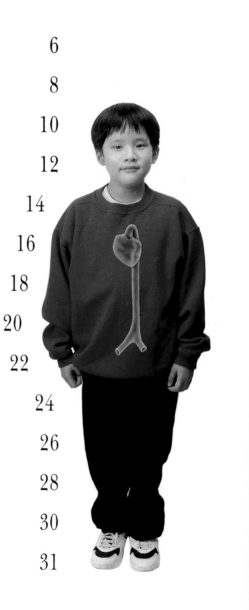

How much blood?

Ouch! You have cut yourself. Blood oozes out of the wound and trickles down your finger. It is bright red. It feels warm and slightly sticky.

If you cut yourself the cut should be cleaned and covered up to stop any germs from getting in. If the cut is small it will heal quickly.

If the cut is very deep then you may need some stitches to hold the cut together until it heals.

When you cut yourself it may feel as if you are losing a lot of blood. But don't worry, you have plenty left. A three-year-old has two pints or more of blood in his or her body – enough to fill a large milk carton; a grown-up has five times this amount. Your body won't notice if it has a few drops less for awhile. In fact, you could lose up to a third of your blood and still survive.

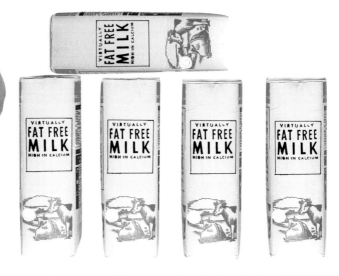

What blood does

Your blood travels around your body like a fast-flowing river.

The blood flowing through your body is known as your bloodstream. It carries the supplies your body needs to grow and stay healthy.

Blood also takes away waste and helps your body to fight off disease and heal wounds.

Heart

Kidneys

Most of your blood is made up of a yellowish liquid called plasma. It takes the nutrients from the food you eat to all parts of your body.

Plasma also takes waste to your kidneys. Your kidneys then filter your blood to take out any waste. You get rid of the waste when you go to the bathroom.

The purified blood goes back into your bloodstream to continue its journey around your body.

Your blood is pumped around your body by the heart. It travels through arteries (shown here in red) and veins (shown here in blue).

Red cell

Blood cells

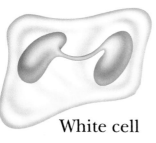 White cell

Floating in the plasma are lots of red cells and white cells. You have many more red cells than white cells. It is your red cells that give your blood its color.

In your lungs red cells take oxygen from the air you breathe and carry it to all parts of your body. As the red cells give up their oxygen, they collect a gas called carbon dioxide, which they take back to your lungs to be breathed out.

In the lungs, blood swaps carbon dioxide for oxygen.

Oxygen

Carbon dioxide

Windpipe

Lung

White cells are much bigger than red cells. Their job is to kill any germs that get into your body. Some germs are so strong they can kill white cells. If your body is attacked by lots of germs, it makes extra white cells to fight them off.

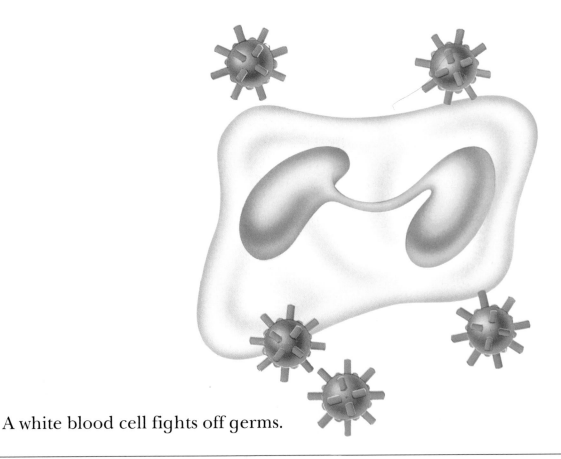

A white blood cell fights off germs.

Cuts and bruises When you cut yourself, blood flows out quickly at first. But unless the cut is very deep, it soon stops.

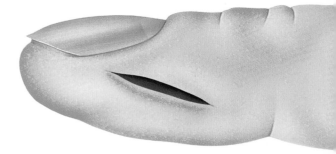

Special repair cells in your blood make a kind of glue, which sticks together tiny drops of blood to form a clot.

The clot acts like a plug to stop any more blood from leaking out. It also stops any germs from getting in. The clot then dries into a scab, which falls off once new skin has grown underneath.

When did you last get a bruise?
How did it happen?

If you bump yourself
hard you get a bruise.
A bruise is formed
because the blood leaks
into your skin and
makes a black-and-blue
mark on the surface.
After a few days the
bruise turns yellow. The
leaked blood is gradually
broken down in the skin
and the bruise
fades away.

The working heart

Your blood is pumped around your body by your heart. Without a heart, your blood would quickly sink into your legs and feet! Your heart began pumping long before you were born. It will go on, day and night, throughout your life.

Your heart is about the size of your fist. Stand straight and place your fingers flat against your chest. Slide them slowly up and down until you feel a throbbing. This is your heart pumping.

Now put your ear against a friend's chest. Listen to the heartbeat. You should be able to hear two sounds for each beat.

Squeeze a ball as hard as you can in one hand. You need strong muscles to do it. Your heart is made of strong muscle. Every time your heart beats it squeezes with enough force to pump your blood out and into your arteries.

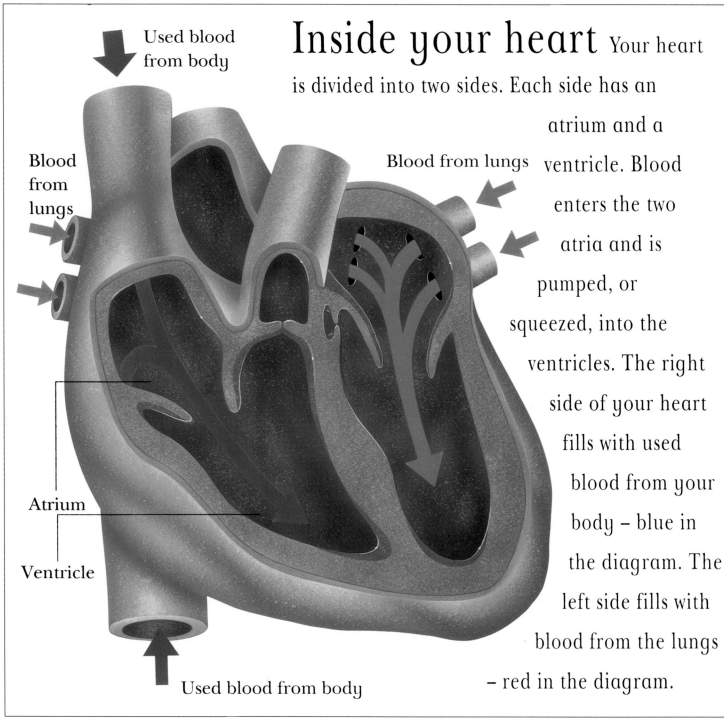

Used blood
from body

Inside your heart
Your heart
is divided into two sides. Each side has an
atrium and a
ventricle. Blood

Blood
from
lungs

Blood from lungs

enters the two

atria and is

pumped, or

squeezed, into the

ventricles. The right

side of your heart

fills with used

blood from your

body – blue in

the diagram. The

left side fills with

blood from the lungs

– red in the diagram.

Atrium

Ventricle

Used blood from body

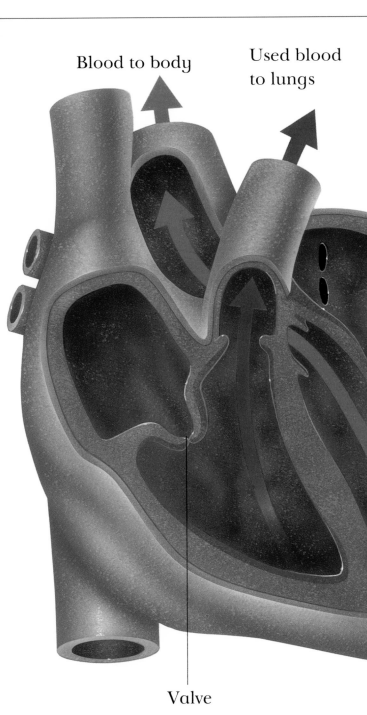

Blood to body

Used blood to lungs

Valve

From here it is pumped into two big blood vessels and out of the heart. The used blood is pumped from the heart to the lungs to collect oxygen. The blood containing oxygen is pumped out of the heart and around your body again.

Between each atrium and ventricle there is a kind of trapdoor called a valve. The valves stop the blood from flowing backward.

Heart

Aorta

Blood vessels

Your blood travels around your body through a network of tubes called blood vessels. The tubes which carry blood away from the heart are called arteries. Those which carry blood back to the heart are called veins. Your aorta is the largest artery in your body. It has thick, elastic walls to move blood along your smaller arteries.

Aorta

Artery

Red cell

Thick, elastic walls

Artery

White cell

Your arteries split into smaller and smaller tubes to reach every part of your body. The smallest tubes are called capillaries. These are just wide enough for one red blood cell to pass through at a time. Look closely at your eye. The red lines you can see are capillaries.

Have you noticed that your face often gets red after you have run a race or played an energetic game? Do you know why this happens?

When you are very hot, your capillaries widen so that more blood can reach the surface of your skin to cool down.

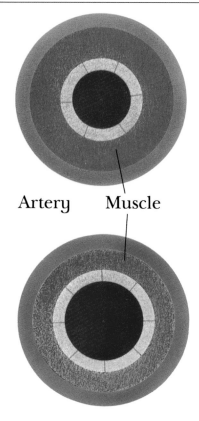

Artery   Muscle

Vein

Your veins

Blood passes from your capillaries into the smallest branches of your veins. Veins are similar to arteries, and the two often lie next to each other. But veins are closer to the surface of the skin. Veins also have narrower, thinner walls than arteries, with only a very thin layer of muscle. Like the heart, they have valves to stop the blood from flowing backward.

Vein

White cell

Red cell

Valve

The blood in your veins has less oxygen in it than the blood in your arteries. This makes it a dull purple-red. Gently bend your hand back and look at your wrist. See how blue your veins look.

Normally, three-fifths of your blood is in your veins. It travels at around eight inches a second. That's about the distance from your wrist to your elbow. In your main arteries, it rushes along at around 12 inches a second.

Your pulse

Every time your heart beats, blood is pushed through your arteries. The blood makes your arteries throb. The speed of the throbs is called your pulse rate. An easy place to feel your pulse is on your wrist. Simply rest the fingertips of one hand just below the thumb of your other hand. How many beats can you feel in one minute?

A grown-up's heart beats about 70 times a minute. A child's heart beats faster. Normally the bigger an animal is, the slower its heartbeat. Compare these ...

Mouse – 600 times a minute

Canary – 800 times a minute

Human infant – 130 times a minute

Adult human –
70 times a minute

If you use up a lot of energy, your heart beats much faster. Try running in place for one minute. Check your pulse to see how many times a minute your heart is beating now.

What other activities make your pulse faster or slower?

Elephant
– 25 times
a minute

Small dog – 120 times a minute

Your heart rate

The number of times your heart beats in one minute is called your heart rate. If you use up a lot of energy, your brain sends a message to your heart, telling it to pump more blood to your muscles. Your heart rate speeds up, and so does your pulse.

If your muscles need it, they can demand over four-fifths of your blood. Usually, they work well on only one fifth.

Your heart rate also increases after you have had a meal. The extra blood is needed to help your digestive system take out the useful parts of the food, called nutrients, and carry them to your liver. Your liver then sorts them out. It stores some and sends most of the rest into your bloodstream and on to your body cells.

Esophagus

Liver

Stomach

Large intestine

Small intestine

The red arrow shows the movement of nutrients from the intestines to the liver. The blood then distributes them around the body.

Blood groups

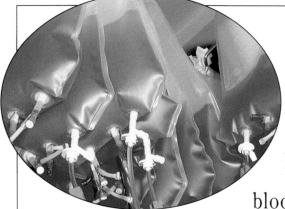

Not everyone's blood is exactly the same. There are four main blood groups - A, B, AB, and O. In some countries, one blood group is much more common than another. Just under half of all the people in the world belong to blood group O.

If someone needs extra blood after an accident or during an operation, doctors have to make sure they give the patient blood that suits their blood group. Someone with blood group A, for example, should not receive group B blood.

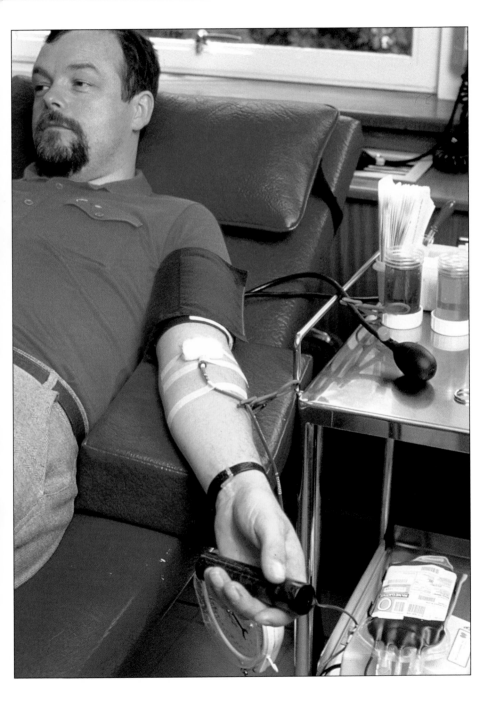

Blood is given to hospitals by blood donors. Any healthy grown-up can donate blood. A nurse pricks a vein and draws out up to one pint of blood. The donor usually notices nothing except the small prick from the needle, and perhaps a little dizziness. The blood is put into a bag and stored in a hospital refrigerator until it is needed.

Did you know?

... that your heart pumps over one gallon (half a bucketful) of blood a minute around your body? That's about 1,500 gallons a day.

... that if you could join all the capillaries in your body they would encircle the world two and a half times?

... that some insects have green blood? Lobsters have blue blood.

... that doctors once used leeches to suck their patients' blood? It was thought to drain sickness from the body.

... that your blood forms about eight per cent of your total body weight?

... that a single drop of blood contains about 100 million red cells and 200,000 white cells?

... that before birth your heart weighed less than one ounce (30 g)? That's half the weight of a chicken's egg. Even a grown-up's heart weighs only about 12 ounces (350 g). Compare that with an elephant's heart, which weighs about 44 pounds (20 kg)!

Glossary

Aorta – The largest artery in your body

Artery – A vessel that carries blood from the heart around the body

Bloodstream – The blood flowing through your body in blood vessels

Heart – The organ that pumps your blood around your body

Plasma – The liquid part of blood

Pulse – The beating of the heart and the arteries that you can feel

Vein – A vessel that carries blood back to your heart from the body

Index